BreeAnn

We wish you God's
favor as you enter a
new phase of life.
May you follow
His leading — Prov. 3:5.6.
Love in the Lord,
Paul & Rachel
Holland

7-2018

WHILE YOU ARE AWAY FROM HOME

BY: MIKE JOHNSON

ENWRIGHTENED
PUBLICATIONS

While You're Away from Home

Copyright © 2013 by Mike Johnson

Cover by: Enwrightened Publications

ISBN-13: 978-1522903246

Enwrightened Publications
P.O. Box 170
Staffordsville, KY 41256
www.enwrightenedpublications.com

Mike Johnson
www.considerthispublications.com

Printed in U.S.A.

This book is dedicated to the Colonels for Christ at Eastern Kentucky University, especially Ben, Jillian, Catie, Erin, Joe, Catelyn, Mike, Bree, Haven, and Brian, with whom I wrote and studied these lessons during the 2009-2010 school year.

CONTENTS

CHAPTER 1
JOSEPH: TAKE GOD WITH YOU

Read the text: Genesis 37:1-36; 39:1-45:28

Joseph was 17 when he was sent away from home. He was around the same age that children are today when they go away from home for college. You ought to be able to identify with him because you know what he was going through in his mind. He was probably scared about what he would find. He was probably unsure of himself and whether he would be able to stay strong. And, I'm sure he missed his dad. His mother had died earlier, (Genesis 36:16-22).

Admittedly, his reason for being away from home was significantly different from yours. His brothers sold him into slavery because they were jealous of him. The Bible records in Genesis 37:4, "But when his brothers saw that their father loved him more than all his brothers, they hated him and could not speak peaceably to him." It is not right for parents to have favorites among their children. At least, it is not right for the children to know that one is favored over the other.

But, Joseph's situation was made even more difficult because he was having visions and dreams that he told to his family. These dreams made it seem that Joseph's family was going to bow down to him someday. His father even rebuked him concerning these dreams, "What is this dream that you have dreamed? Shall your mother and I and your brothers indeed come to bow down to the earth before you?" (Genesis 37:16)

To make the situation even worse in the sight of Joseph's brothers, Jacob, their father, gave Joseph a tunic, or coat, of colors, (Genesis 37:3). Additionally, Joseph had given a bad report about them to their father, (Genesis 37:2). There is no indication of what the bad report was, but it seems that it had something to do with how they acted. All of these things added up to a recipe for trouble. The hatred of the brothers for Joseph finally boiled over and they sold him into slavery, sending him to Egypt, (Genesis 37:18-36).

Joseph was in a foreign land, seemingly through no fault of his own, and certainly because of his brothers' hatred and jealousy. He could have responded in a rebellious and angry way. No one would have blamed him if he had. However, Joseph turned the situation into a positive one and he became, eventually, second-in-command in Egypt. And, the brothers fulfilled the dreams he had had as a young boy as they bowed down to Joseph as a ruler of Egypt. So, how was Joseph able to be so successful? He took God with him when he went away from home.

Joseph Stood With God (Genesis 39:1-9)

In a far away land, Joseph faced a temptation that was just like the temptations that young people face today while they are away from home. He was a trusted slave in the household of an Egyptian captain of the guard. The Bible records that Joseph was "a successful man..." (v. 2). The reason for this is that "...the Lord was with him and...made all he did to prosper in his hand." (v. 3).

The temptation he faced came from the wife of his master. Apparently, she had focused on Joseph for a while and wanted a sexual relationship with him. The text declares that she "...cast longing eyes..." on him even approaching him with the words, "Lie with me." (v. 7). Temptations into sexual activity are common among young people who go away from home. These temptations are not easy to turn down. Joseph was away from home. No one knew him. He could do this without anyone from back home knowing anything about it.

This is the danger of these temptations. When you are away from home and those that know you, it is easier to convince yourself that you can participate in activities you would not at home simply because no one in this place knows you. However, learn the lesson that Joseph knew. In his refusal of the temptation, he revealed the key to conquering it. He said to the woman, "How, then, can I do this great wickedness and sin against God?" (v. 9).

Joseph was not thinking about his family or friends back home when he turned down the temptation. He was thinking about the one Being who did know what he was doing in this far away place.

He Stood Up for God (Genesis 41:16)

The fallout from his refusal of Potiphar's wife landed him in jail. At least two years passed with Joseph in an Egyptian prison. While there, he met two men that each had a dream they did not understand. Joseph, with the Lord's help, gave the interpretation leading to the opportunity to interpret a dream for the Pharaoh.

The Pharaoh's dream upset him mightily. His butler was one of the men for whom Joseph had interpreted a dream, telling him that he would be released from prison and return to his job serving the Pharaoh. He had forgotten about Joseph, but was reminded of him when the Pharaoh was searching for someone to interpret his dream. He convinced the Pharaoh to call Joseph to interpret the dream.

The Pharaoh called Joseph and said to him, "I have had a dream and there is no one who can interpret it. But I have heard it said of you that you can understand a dream, to interpret it" (v. 15). In this statement, there was the temptation to his ego. He could have used this opportunity to get something out of the Pharaoh. But, his words show the motivation behind his entire life, "It is not in me; God will give Pharaoh an answer of peace" (v. 16).

In this far away land, Joseph did not seek to gain material possessions or fame for himself. The driving force of his life was to stand up for God, giving Him the glory and credit for all good things in Joseph's life. While you are away from home, look for opportunities to give glory to God, letting people know that you are on His side fully.

He Stood by God (Genesis 45:5-7)

The Pharaoh's dream came to pass just as Joseph had said. In the intervening years, (at least 14), Joseph was second-in-command in Egypt and in charge of meeting the challenges that the dream had foretold. For the first seven years, the land in Egypt brought forth plentifully. Joseph stored up grain for the coming seven years of famine. The wide-spread famine eventually brought Joseph's family to Egypt in search of food. They bowed before Joseph, not knowing who he was, thereby fulfilling his childhood dreams.

Here was Joseph's opportunity. His brothers, who had sold him into slavery and lied to his father about his death, were bowing before him. He could have had their heads removed from their bodies. He could banish them to the same prison that had held him for so long. Their fate and their lives were in his hands. However, he did not react as many others might have. He verified, again, that his most important possession in that far away land was the Lord he took with him there.

He revealed himself to his brothers who now were scared for their lives. But, Joseph's words showed that he was still standing by God, as he had been ever since his arrival in the far away place. He said, "...God sent me before you to preserve life...and God sent me before you to preserve a posterity for you in the earth, and to save your lives by a great deliverance" (Genesis 45:5-7).

While you are away from home, be sure to take God with you. He should be the first possession that you pack as you prepare to leave. He should be the first you unpack as you arrive in the new place. He should be with you in the Bible you carry and study. He should be with you in constant prayer. He should be with you as you find the brothers and sisters in your spiritual family and assemble with them for worship and fellowship.

Prayer: *Oh Lord, I thank You that You have been with me my entire life. I had my family, friends, and church family back home. Now, I am away from them and am facing life on my own for the first time. I don't want to let them down and I sure don't want to let You down. I ask You to be with me. Give me Your strength to overcome the temptations that I will face. Stay with me and help me to stay with You. You are my strength and my shield. Be my ever present help in time of need. In the name of Jesus', Amen.*

Brainstorming Ideas to Make this a Reality in Your Life:
1. Be vocal about your Christianity. Let others know that you intend to live this way.

2. Know what your particular temptations are and put up roadblocks to them that will make it harder to give in. (Stay away from places where you know you will be tempted.)

3. Carry a Bible with you wherever you go. It will be a reminder to you of the proper way to live.

4. Begin every day with prayer. Pray all day.

5. Thank your parents for showing you who God is and helping to put Him into your life.

What other ideas do you have?
1.
2.
3.

Discussion Starters:

1. What are some things you were apprehensive about before leaving home? How were these concerns or fears dealt with?

2. What are some other temptations that could possibly steer us away from the things God want us to do? How can we avoid them?

3. Dating is a typical part of the college years. How can we retain a good Christian relationship and not lose our sexual purity when we find that special person?

4. How can we let others see God in our lives as we walk around campus and hang out with our friends? Would this be easier or harder at home?

5. Think of an instance when you could have used the line "I told you so", but instead you "killed them with kindness". Which reaction makes you feel better in the end?

6. Discuss a time when you might have wanted to leave God at home, but when the situation played out you sure were glad He was there to help you.

7. Do you think it would hurt worse to hurt your friends' feelings by not going out clubbing with them or telling your boyfriend/girlfriend that you are not having sex with them or to disappoint your parents and God by turning your back on what you know is right?

8. Did your parents give you a bunch of "do's" and "don'ts" before you left home? How did you feel about those expectations?

9. If you hadn't already located a congregation to worship with before starting school, were you worried about finding a good sound church? Why?

While You Are Away From Home

CHAPTER 2
ABRAM: TRUST GOD EXPLICITLY

Read the Text: Genesis 12:1-25:11

Explicit trust in God means that others can see that trust. It is clear and obvious in your actions and in your decisions. It is not merely an implicit trust. That is, it is not a trust that is implied or behind the scenes. It is public trust. Those who trust God explicitly leave a trail of evidence that others can see clearly.

While you are away from home, you, too, should trust God explicitly; don't leave others wondering whether you do or not. Don't hide your trust. Don't be ashamed of your trust in God. It should be so obvious that others will not have to question where your trust lies. Abram is a great example of one who trusted God during the most critical times of his life as he left behind his home to go to a brand new country.

Trust God to Lead You in a Good Path

Your first call to leave home and go out on your own usually comes after you have completed high school. It can seem like a sudden and dramatic break from all that you have known for your whole life. While you are probably very excited to be leaving, you may not be as clear what direction your life will take. All of a sudden, you have to decide your major in college and the school you will go to. You need to pick your classes, decide about a roommate, and get things together for your room. It is a whirlwind time!

Maybe you are experiencing some anxiety about the direction of your life. It is natural in this time not to have a totally clear vision of the direction of your life. We have all been through it and we all can relate to what you are going through. Abram is a great example of one whose direction in life was rather unclear.

God appeared to him in Genesis 12 and told him, "Get out of your country, from your family, and from your father's house to a land that I will show you" (verse 1). God was not very specific about the direction Abram was to head. Abram was not given a clearly marked map showing the route he was going to take and the eventual destination of that trip. He had to trust that God was leading him on a good path to a good destination. His trust in God led him to do exactly as God had said. He picked up, packed up, and headed out.

The direction of your life is not set specifically. There will be twists and turns. There will be obstacles that need to be overcome and there will be setbacks, some caused by your own poor choices and some caused by the poor choices of others. However, there is one thing that you can count on. As long as you put your trust in God, He will never lead you in a poor direction. You may not see, at every turn, what the next station will bring, but you can rest assured that the journey will be worth your effort and patience in the end. Abram found this to be true and you will, too.

Trust God to Fulfill All of His Promises

God's call to Abram had a second part: "I will make you a great nation; I will bless you and make your name great; and you shall be a blessing. I will bless those who bless you and I will curse him who curses you; and in you all the families of the earth shall be blessed" (verses 2-3). There were two issues that Abram could have chosen to concentrate on rather than trusting in God. First, Sarai, his wife, was barren, (Genesis 11:30). This was a blow to both of them. In their society, a woman felt totally incomplete if she did not give birth to a child. (For evidence of this see Genesis 30:1 where Rachel, Jacob's wife who was barren, said to him, "Give me children, or else I die!") The fact that they did not have a child could, also, have been a temptation for Abram to doubt the promise of God, who said that He would bless all nations through his offspring. Yet, Abram remained faithful.

The second problem was the age of Abram and Sarai. Not only was Sarai barren, but she was old enough not to have any reason to expect that things would change. And, Abram was no young man! He was 75 when God called him, (Genesis 12:4). His own father started having children when he was 70 years old (Genesis 11:26). Abram could have surmised that his time to have children had come and gone. But, he never wavered.

The events that follow may appear to be evidence that Abram did not have faith in God's promises. However, they actually show exactly the opposite. Even though he did not act properly, his actions grew out of his full trust in God.

Abram's natural curiosity finally led him to ask God about the promise. "Lord God, what will You give me, seeing I go childless, and the heir of my house is Eliezer of Damascus? Look, You have given me no offspring; indeed one born in my house is my heir!'(Genesis 15:2-3). Abram did not distrust God; he was merely trying to read God's method for accomplishing what He had promised! His statement was his way of saying, "Is this what You meant?"

The Lord responded, "This one shall not be your heir, but one who will come from your own body shall be your heir" (Genesis 15:4). This second piece of the unfolding promise led to the next trust-inspired wrong turn. He and Sarai agreed that Abram, from his own body, could have a child through Hagar, Sarai's maid, (Genesis 16). They did have that child, but that was not the fulfillment of God's promise.

Now, God gave the final piece of the puzzle. He spoke to Abram, (whom He now named "Abraham", Genesis 17:1-8) and to Sarai (whom He now named "Sarah", Genesis 17:15) and said, "I will bless her and also give you a son by her; then I will bless her, and she shall be a mother of nations; kings of peoples shall be from her" (Genesis 17:16). Now, the promise was clear. Abraham and Sarah would have a child of their own! Abram never doubted God, though he did attempt to help God's plan along.

While you are away from home, do not doubt that God will do just as He has promised. He has promised not to allow you to be tempted beyond what you can bear, but will provide a way of escape for you, (1 Corinthians 10:13). He has promised that if you seek His will you will find it, (Matthew 7:7). He has promised peace in times of difficulty if you look for it, (Philippians 4:6-7). And, don't ever doubt His overall promise of Heaven for the faithful, (John 14:1-4). Abraham is living proof that we can trust God explicitly in every one of His promises.

Trust God to Make Possible What Seems Impossible

It must have seemed impossible to Abraham and Sarah that they would have a child. But, that was nothing compared to what was coming next. This final event shows the depth of Abraham's trust in God. He was 100 years old when he received the fulfillment of God's promise and had Isaac, (Genesis 21:1-7). Abraham may have thought that his life had finally settled down. He had left his home and traveled to a distant land. He had experienced God's promise of a son. Could there be any more tests of his trust? Hadn't he been tested enough?

"Now it came to pass after these things that God tested Abraham, and said to him, 'Abraham!' And he said, 'Here I am.' Then He said, 'Take now your son, your only son Isaac, whom you love, and go to the land of Moriah, and offer him there as a burnt offering on one of the mountains of which I shall tell you" (Genesis 22:1-2). We might have been tempted to say, if all this had happened to us, "Are you kidding me? I have waited all this time for my son. I have done everything You have asked. And now, You want me to offer him as a sacrifice? I don't think that is fair!"

Abraham, however, was not of that nature. The very next verse says, "So Abraham rose early in the morning and saddled his donkey…" (Genesis 22:3). He did not waver even a little bit. He went to the mountain intending to offer his son upon an altar he would build. How could he do this? Isn't that a cruel thing to ask and an even more cruel thing to set out to do? But, it is in this test that we see the greatest evidence of Abraham's trust in God. Hebrews 11:17-19 records, "By faith Abraham, when he was tested, offered up Isaac, and he who had received the promises offered up his only begotten son, of whom it was said, 'In Isaac your seed shall be called,' concluding that God was able to raise him up, even from the dead, from which he also received him in a figurative sense."

There is the crowning moment in Abraham's trust in God. He had already decided that if he sacrificed Isaac on the altar God would raise him from the dead and give him back! Now, that is powerful trust!

No one knows what lies ahead in life. However, we can know that God will be there to help even when things seem impossible. You may get over your head in some tragedy or mishap. You may feel like the weight of the world is crashing down on you. You may not see a way out of what seems to be an impossible situation. But, there is one thing you can know and do: "Trust in the Lord with all your heart, and lean not on your own understanding; in all your ways acknowledge Him, and He shall direct your paths" (Proverbs 3:5).

The life-lesson of the life of Abraham is to trust God explicitly. While you are away from home, lean heavily on this truth. And remember, part of trusting in God is trusting in His people who also trust in Him. Get advice and counsel from others who trust God when you get in trouble. But, never turn your back on Him!

Prayer: *Heavenly Father, I want to thank You for always being there for me. You have never let me down, even though I have let You down often. I want to assure You of my trust and ask that You help me follow through. Help me to focus on Your promises and Your help during the difficult times of my life. Give me enough success*

While You Are Away From Home

to strengthen my faith and enough difficulty to test it and keep it strong. In Jesus' name, Amen.

Brainstorming Ideas to Make this a Reality in Your Life:

1. Make a list of times that were difficult and the solutions that you found.

2. Listen to someone's story about trusting God and finding Him to be true.

3. Pray that you will know the will of God when you get into difficult situations.

What other ideas do you have?
1.
2.
3.

Discussion Starters:

1. Why is it hard to trust God to lead us in a good path?

2. How have you seen God's promise fulfilled in your life?

3. What things can you do to learn to trust in God completely?

While You Are Away From Home

CHAPTER 3
NAAMAN'S JEWISH SERVANT GIRL : ACT LIKE YOU'RE STILL AT HOME

Read the text: II Kings 5:1-19

It was an unstable time in the history of the Israelite people. The Moabites from the south were in rebellion against Israel, (II Kings 3) and the Syrians from the north were raiding the perimeter, (II Kings 5). The story of the Jewish slave girl begins with one of these raids. This un-named girl from Israel was kidnapped and taken to the land of Syria to be the slave of the commander of the army, Naaman, (II Kings 5:1-2). He was "a great and honorable man" and "a mighty man of valor" (verse 1). His master put much faith in him because the hand of the Lord was on him as he led the people to victory.

This man, however, had a debilitating disease. He was a leper. Thus, he was an outcast, even though he was a hero. This was a highly contagious disease forcing those infected to live away from family and friends until such a time that they were disease-free, an unlikely scenario, at best. But, the Lord was guiding the situation.

Here is where we meet the Jewish slave girl. She had been as-signed to wait on Naaman's wife. As a slave, she would have been ex-pected to do many chores and be on constant vigil to attend to the needs and desires of her master. She seems to have been sympathetic toward Naaman, moving her to reveal that she knows how he can be cured, (II Kings 5:3). This news was unbelievable! Could this slave girl really know where to find the cure for leprosy?

Why did she treat them with such kindness? Why did she not lash out against her captors? Why did she not rebel and refuse to work? What motivated her to live in this situation, seemingly, without anger and resentment? The key is that while she was away from home, she contin-ued to act as though she were still at home.

You need to honor the values your parents and family have taught you while you are away from home. They have invested their lives in training and disciplining you to live independently. In the process, they have passed on to you those values and morals that are important to them and that they hope are important to you. The slave girl in this story had some basic values she had learned from her family and they are worthy of your consideration while you are away from yours.

She Did Not Blame God for the Bad Things in Her Life

Apparently, this young girl had been well-trained at home not to blame God for her troubles. She and her family had experienced some very severe troubles. They had lived in fear of the nations outside of the border of Israel. They probably had heard about the raids from those heathen nations and lived in fear that the same would happen to them.

And, then, the unthinkable happened! A raid took this young girl to a far away land away from her home and family. There is no mention of the fate of her family. Were they killed in the raid, leaving her alone? Had they escaped thinking that she was with other family members? Had they, too, been taken into captivity in another place? We just do not know what happened to them. But, we do know this: they raised a principled daughter. It is clear that this family did not blame God for the bad things that were happening all around them.

Her time as a child in the home of her family, (we do not know how old she was), taught her this very important lesson. God is not responsible for the difficulties of life. Sure, God does discipline His people, (Hebrews 12:3-11). However, He does not tempt His people to sin, (James 1:12-18).

And, He is not blind to our troubles and suffering. The troubles of life can direct us back onto the proper pathway from which we may have strayed. Sometimes, these troubles are the result of our own poor choices, leaving us to suffer because of them. Others are the result of the choices of others and we suffer innocently. But, the God of Heaven is not blind to our suffering. He admonishes us, "Therefore humble yourselves under the mighty hand of God, that He may exalt you in due time, casting all your care upon Him, for He cares for you" (I Peter 5:6-7).

You will experience many difficulties while you are away from home. But, live as though you are still at home and refuse to blame God for these troubles. Your parents did not teach you to do that. They taught you to respect God, even during difficult times.

She Did What She was Told to Do

These people had ripped her from her family and home and still she did what she was supposed to do. Obviously, she had been raised to obey those who were in authoritative positions over her. Even though she was not at her home, she still believed that the lessons she had learned about her place with respect to those in authority was still in effect. If she were still at home, she would be under the authority of her family. While she was away from home, she honored her family by remaining true to this basic principle of life.

You will never have a time in your life that you are totally free of any authority over you. And, that applies to your time in college. You probably have thought, at some time in the recent past, about how great it will be to be on your own. If you are going to college, you may be thinking about the freedom you will have away from your parents' harassment about chores, clean rooms, and curfews. But, you will still have deadlines and demands from someone over you in your program of study.

If you are leaving home to go into the work force, you certainly will be in a submissive situation as someone over you assigns you the work that you are to do. You will have traded the authority of parents for the authority of a boss, (and you will come, very soon, to appreciate even more the greater freedom you had under your parents!).

She Cared About Those Who Had Put Her in Slavery

The Jews had been called by God to be His special people. Many Jews became arrogant because of this and saw themselves superior to every other person. Many of them even grew to hate anyone who was a Gentile. There was great animosity between Jews and Gentiles.

The actions of this young girl to her Gentile captors show the kind of teaching she had received while she was at home. When she had the opportunity, she showed her real attitude toward someone in need. She cared about her master's health. She shared the good news about the prophet who had the power to heal even this dreaded disease, (II Kings 5:3). To those who had mistreated her, taking her from her parents, she did a good deed showing the kind of teaching she had received from her family.

While you are away from home, make sure that you care, even about those who make fun of you and seek to do you harm. Being good to those who are not good to you is the real test of character. "For if you love those who love you, what reward have you?" (Matthew 5:46)

Most people love those who love them. But, loving our enemies is not easy. Yet, that is exactly what God expects, "But I say to you, love your enemies, bless those who curse you, do good to those who hate you, and pray for those who spitefully use you and persecute you" (Matthew 5:44).

These are three powerful lessons that this young servant girl teaches us about how to act and how to live while we are away from home. If she could do what she did, you can do it, too. While you are away from home, live as though you are still at home.

Prayer: *Dear God and Father, thank You for the life You have given me. I know that I will face my share of difficulties and troubles, but I pray that You will help me not to allow them to give me a negative attitude. I pray that I will treat everyone as I want to be treated, even those who do me wrong. I also ask for your patience as I learn to live by these principles. Give me enough trouble to appreciate the good times of life and enough good times to have confidence to live through the bad times. In Jesus' name, Amen.*

Brainstorming Ideas to Make this a Reality in Your Life:

1. Plan to do a good deed for someone you do not know or, even better, someone you do not like.

2. Identify some troubles in your life and what you can learn from going through them properly.

3. Write a thank-you note to someone who helped you go through some difficulty.

4. Thank your parents for the way that they helped you learn to handle troubles without blaming God.

What other ideas do you have?
1.
2.
3.

Discussion Starters:

1. Why are so many people so willing to blame God for the problems in their lives?

2. Why do you think some people have trouble being submissive to those in authority? Does being submissive make a person less human or something?

3. Jesus told us to love our enemies. Why is it so difficult and how can you do a better job of it?

4. How would you help someone who was not raised in a home that gave them good principles to live by?

While You Are Away From Home

CHAPTER 4
MORDECAI: BE A PERSON OF VALUES

Read the Text: Esther 10:3

Both Mordecai and Esther were away from home. They had lived in Babylon ever since their homeland was invaded by the Babylonian empire, (Ester 2:5-6). Babylon had now, in turn, been overrun by the Medes and Persians. Ahasuerus was the king and he was looking for a new queen after he had dismissed the previous one for insubordination. He summoned many women to the capital to be prepared to compete to be the queen. Over time, Esther won the honor and her uncle, Mordecai, who had raised her from infancy, stayed nearby to guide and look out for his niece.

The Old Testament book of Esther bears the name of the famous Jewish queen to King Ahasuerus of the Persia empire. However, the book closes with a couple of verses praising the one who might be the real hero of the book, Mordecai. "Now all the acts of his power and his might, and the account of the greatness of Mordecai, to which the king advanced him, are they not written in the book of the chronicles of the kings of Media and Persia? For Mordecai the Jew was second to King Ahasuerus, and was great among the Jews and well received by the multitude of his brethren, seeking the good of his people and speaking peace to all his countrymen" (Esther 10:2-3).

Mordecai's time away from home is a study in the importance of personal values. He left a legacy of greatness because he was faithful to the values he had brought with him into this foreign land. These values are clear and proper. As you are away from home, you need these same values. You need to be a principled person. You need your own value system that is consistent with the Word of God and that you will follow, no matter what may come your way.

He Valued His Religion

That closing verse of the book of Esther said that Mordecai was, "great among the Jews". The Jewish nation was a theocracy; that is, they were governed directly by God. He gave them their law, He raised up their judges and their first 3 kings, and He sent prophets who tried to bring them back to faithfulness when they strayed. Jewish life and Jewish religion were practically one in the same.

Mordecai valued life, even the life of the man under whom he was a captive. Moses had commanded the Jews, "…but you shall love your neighbor as yourself." (Leviticus 19:18) The Jews never seemed to understand this commandment very well. They loved their Jewish neighbors, but they did not love their gentile neighbors. Mordecai could not just stand by and listen to a plot to murder the king without doing something, (Esther 2:21-23). His religious values, based on the law of Moses, just would not allow him to do that.

Mordecai valued God above every man. Though Mordecai valued the life of Ahasuerus, he did not value anyone or anything more than the God of Heaven. The king's second-in-command, Haman, was a man swelled by the power of his position. Everywhere he went, the people bowed before him because of his closeness to the king. Mordecai, however, did not bow, (Esther 3:1-2). Apparently, everyone else did. Yet, the only thing Haman saw was the one who did not. Mordecai's refusal to bow was reason enough for Haman to plot to kill all the Jews. Mordecai valued what Jesus referred to as the greatest command: "You shall love the LORD your God with all your heart, with all your soul, and with all your strength" (Deuteronomy 6:5).

Mordecai valued God's providential care. When Mordecai was made aware of Haman's plot to kill all the Jews, he appealed to Esther to intercede for the people. She was hesitant, as the new queen, because of the king's policy that only those bidden to him could come to him in full assurance that they would not be killed. Anyone else who took the chance was subject to the wrath of the king. Mordecai convinced Esther with these words, "Yet who knows whether you have come to the kingdom for such a time as this?" (Esther 4:14) Though he does not mention God specifically, it is clear that he trusts that God is still in charge, no matter what plot Haman might devise.

These three values summarize what faithfulness to God is all about: love God above all else with your whole life, love your neighbor as yourself, and trust that God is charge over the affairs of the world. You, too, should value your religion that tells you these same things.

While You Are Away From Home

He Valued His Reputation

Esther 10:3 records about Mordecai that he was "well received by the multitude of his brethren". Mordecai had a good reputation among his Jewish brethren. There were probably many reasons why this was true; two of which can be gleaned by observing his life. He had a reputation of being helpful by his actions in behalf of Esther, (Esther 2:10, 20). His advice to Esther about what not to say was helpful, both to her and to their brethren.

Mordecai was also a humble man. He had thwarted the plot to kill the king, (Esther 2:21-23. However, he did not do it to gain fame and wealth. According to the king's record in Esther 6:1-3, nothing had ever been done to reward him for that deed. Mordecai had not sought payment or prestige for his heroic act. After he received a reward from the king, (Esther 6:4-11), Mordecai returned to his customary place at the king's gate to be available to help Esther if ever she needed him again.

While you are away from home, you should strive to have a good reputation. You should remember the words of the wise in Proverbs 22:1, "A good name should be chosen than great riches." Mordecai certainly understood this. A good reputation cannot be bought with money. It can only be bought through hard and consistent work.

He Valued Responsibility

Mordecai valued responsibility. Those last words of the book of Esther commend him for "seeking the good of his people". The whole book of Esther might be described in terms of Mordecai's responsibility. The book opens describing Mordecai's responsibility to his family. Esther had been orphaned. Both of her parents had died. "Mordecai took her as his own daughter." (Esther 2:7) There seems to have been no deep thought about the matter. She did not have her parents anymore and Mordecai took the responsibility on himself. He brought her up, (Esther 2:20), to value the same things that he did, for she joined with him in the great story that unfolds in this great book.

Mordecai also valued his responsibility to his people. When he learned of the plot against his people, it was clear that he had to act. As of yet, Esther had not heard of the plot. Mordecai was now ready to reveal his own nationality and encouraged Esther to take the lead before the king, informing him of the impending doom on her people. His concern was not merely personal. His was a concern about the nation. He trusted that help would come from some source, (Esther 4:13-14). However, he knew that he and Esther were in a unique position to help.

It was, therefore, their responsibility to do so.

The great temptation to those who are away from home is to be irresponsible. Sometimes it seems easy to live that way because no one around knows you like people do back home. But, responsibility does not change with a change of address. You have the same responsibilities while you are away as you do when you are home. You should still honor your family. You still honor your friends and others when they are in need. Responsibility is not always easy. However, it is always necessary.

He Valued Relationships

Mordecai valued his relationships. The final thing said about Mordecai in the book is a commendation for "speaking peace to all his countrymen". We have already seen how important it was to him to take care of his family. He had maintained such a good relationship with Esther that it is said of her that she "obeyed the command of Mordecai as when she was brought up by him" (Esther 2:20). It was important for him to stay close to Esther her whole life.

He valued his relationships as a Jewish man. He led the effort to help his brethren be strong enough to fight against their enemies. He inspired and encouraged them so well that they won a great victory, killing more than 75,000 who rose up against them, (Esther 9:16).

Mordecai also valued relationships with others. With Mordecai leading the way, the Jews won a great military victory. However, they did not plunder the goods of the conquered. Esther 9:10 and 15 both mention this fact. It is a curious fact in the midst of a great battle. It could be expected that if you win a battle, you are allowed to have the plunder of goods from those who intended to do you harm. However, this was not what Mordecai, evidently, led them to do. Their refusal to take the goods of the people left them with an opportunity to maintain a good relationship with the people of the land, for they could not be accused of greed. Their actions, in fact, affected the people of the land positively, "then many of the people of the land became Jews, because fear of the Jews fell upon them" (Esther 8:17).

While you are away from home, remember the value of good relationships. Maintain a good relationship with your family. Work to have good relationships with people in your new place of residence. And, find the family of God where you are. There is no more important relationship that you can develop than that of being with the people of God, working with them to do the things of God.

Prayer: *Oh Lord. I want to ask you to help me develop positive relationships for my life. I realize that my relationships with others can contribute to my destruction or to my success. Help me appreciate all that my family has done for me all these years. Give me strength to have relationships with people who are not Your children and lead them to You. Please give me a strong Christian church family to be with while I am away from my Christian family back home. I pray that others will be influenced for good by the way I interact with the people in my life. In Jesus' name, Amen.*

Brainstorming Ideas to Make this a Reality in Your Life:

1. Write a letter, send an email, or make a phone call to various family members while you are away, letting them know that you are thinking of them and love them.

2. Make it a habit to go to places where good people hang out in order to find good friends.

3. Attend various church fellowship functions and try to make connections with people in that local congregation.

What other ideas do you have?
1.
2.
3.

Discussion Starters:

1. Why do people often lose contact with family members and close friends while they are away from home?

2. How do good friends help you and keep you on the straight and narrow pathway? What is the meaning of 1 Corinthians 15:33?

3. How does a person go about finding and developing new friendships?

4. List some good friend relationships in Scripture.

5. List some bad friend relationships in Scripture.

While You Are Away From Home

CHAPTER 5
TIMOTHY: MAINTAIN YOUR GOOD REPUTATION

Read The Text: Acts 16:1-5; Philippians 2:19-24

Timothy was a young man who grew up in Lystra. He had learned the truth of the gospel from his Jewish mother, Eunice, and grandmother, Lois, (II Timothy 1:5). It seems likely that they learned the Gospel the first time Paul came to the city, (Acts 14:8-18). Though his father was Greek, Timothy pursued the Christian lifestyle of his mother and grandmother. His practice of Christianity was well-known, even to the other two near-by cities Derbe and Iconium, (Acts 16:1-2). It was this solid reputation among the area Christians that convinced Paul to take Timothy with him and make him a part of his evangelistic efforts. Apparently, Timothy traveled with Paul from that time on.

When Timothy was away from home, he took with him that reputation. Whatever he did in the future would enhance or diminish that reputation. Furthermore, whatever he did would be a reflection of those who had any part in teaching him. His reputation was, therefore, a reflection of his family and friends. Maybe, as he left, his mother told him the same thing I remember my dad telling me on more than one occasion. He said, "Son, remember that you are wearing my name. Whatever you do will not only say something about you, it will also say something about me and your mother."

Timothy had a responsibility while he was away from home to keep his reputation intact. It is an interesting thing about a reputation. You can take many years building it into something that you can be proud of, yet you can damage it deeply in just a few moments of time. It is harder to build a reputation than it is to destroy one. But, that is true of anything. It is always easier to tear something down than to build it up. It is important, therefore, that you be on guard of your reputation every moment. Timothy is a great study of one who guarded his reputation well.

Philippians 2:19-24 provides three keys to maintaining your reputation. This text is Paul's verification that Timothy maintained his reputation throughout the years that he worked with Paul. He provides us insight into Timothy's character, showing us three ways that Timothy worked to keep his reputation at a high level.

Timothy was Sincere

Paul intended to send Timothy to the church in Philippi, so that he might report how well the church was doing. Paul said, "For I have no one like-minded, who will sincerely care for your state." Timothy maintained his good reputation because he was sincere in what he did. No one appreciates a hypocrite. We don't want to be admonished and rebuked by someone who is doing the very things he is telling us not to do. Timothy followed the Lord sincerely. Everyone knew of his sincerity and trusted him because of it. Timothy's reputation remained exemplary for this reason.

It is important for you to be sincere in your interactions with others. Be what your good reputation is built upon. Sincerity demands honesty. Honesty is the cornerstone of sincerity. It is dishonest to portray yourself one way while you are, in fact, not that at all. You might be tempted at times to be a different person, thinking that it is necessary in order to fit in. However, that kind of deception costs you much more in the future when people learn who you really are. As the folks of generations ago were fond of saying, don't put on airs. Also, be willing to admit when you are wrong. This will add to your reputation as a sincere individual.

Timothy was Selfless

"For all seek their own, not the things which are of Christ Jesus" (verse 21). Selfless people think of others before they think of themselves. One of the best ways to maintain a good reputation is to be a selfless individual. Those who busy themselves looking out for the welfare of others will never suffer from a poor reputation. Those who pursue a path that puts others first will never need to be concerned about a damaged reputation.

As you step out into your own life for the first time, you will face the challenges of selfishness. You are forming your own life away from the intense guidance you have lived under your whole life. Now, you get to manage your life with less management from parents, family, and other important people who have been there for you and with you for many years. You have embarked on a journey in which you have greater control.

The temptations to selfishness will come in many forms. If you are pursuing education leading to a career, you might be tempted to focus so hard on your goals that you will have no time for others and their needs will go unnoticed. Remember, while you are reaching for your career goals, don't forget that loving your neighbor as yourself is the second greatest command according to Jesus, (Matthew 22:39). Be an active part of the church wherever you are. That connection will give you opportunities to remember and help the plight of others. You will hear about those who are sick and suffering in many ways. Active participation in the church while you are away will keep you in touch with people in need and help keep you from being exclusively inwardly-focused.

Timothy was a Servant

Timothy's life was an example of service. It began as he left his home and dedicated himself to travel with Paul through all of his missionary journeys. Paul referred to him as his fellow worker, (Romans 16:21; I Thessalonians 3:2). He had ministered to Paul in Macedonia, (Acts 19:22). He represented Paul before the Corinthians, (I Corinthians 4:17) and the Thessalonians, (I Thessalonians 3:6), until Paul could make another personal appearance there. He even spent time in prison because of his service to the Lord that made him a target of many who did not want Christianity to flourish, (Hebrews 13:23).

While you are away from home, don't bypass opportunities to serve others. Serving yourself is really easy. You may even have said or thought before you left how glad you were to be leaving home so you could do whatever you wanted to do.

However, a sincerely selfless person will not serve only himself. Look for doors of service you can open. Volunteer, organize, and create ways to help those in need. Through the church where you are, you will learn of people who need your help. If you are in college, there are many community service opportunities. There is no greater reputation than to be known as a servant to all. Jesus' reputation that Peter proclaimed to Cornelius was that He "went about doing good", (Acts 10:38). Let His example and reputation inspire you while you are away from home.

Prayer: *Our Father in Heaven, I praise Your great name. Thank you for the training I have had from family and friends. Please help me to live up to their expectations of me. I don't want to disappoint them and damage my reputation in their sight. Please help me to have a sincere heart, a selfless attitude, and servant hands. Open doors of opportunity through which I may develop these things more deeply in my life. And, remind me who I am and Whose I am. In Jesus' name, Amen.*

Brainstorming Ideas to Make this a Reality in Your Life:

1. Determine to do an act of service for someone on a regular basis.

2. Do an act of service that no one ever knows about.

3. Invite someone else to do a service with you in order to spread the servant mentality.

4. Thank your parents for the good reputation they have and, therefore, have imparted to you.

What other ideas do you have?
1.
2.
3.

Discussion Starters:

1. What are some other ways to be a servant to those in need?

2. Discuss a time when you were a servant to those in need and describe how it made you feel spiritually.

3. How do you think people view your reputation?

4. If you feel your reputation isn't as good as it could be, what are some ways to correct it?

5. How would someone know by looking at your life that you are sincere about your Christian lifestyle away from home?

While You Are Away From Home

6. What are some ways to balance good selfishness and bad selfishness?

7. How can you keep optimistic about helping others when it is not convenient?

8. What was happening the last time your reputation was in danger?

9. What are some things your family and friends told you about maintaining your reputation before you left home?

While You Are Away From Home

CHAPTER 6
DANIEL : DEVELOP GOOD HABITS

Read the Text: Daniel 1:1-21; 6:1-28

Daniel was away from his home, but not by his own choosing. He was part of the group of people taken into captivity by Nebuchadnezzar during the reign of Jehoiakim, King of Judah, (Daniel 1:1). He was brought there for very specific reasons. King Nebuchadnezzar had instructed Ashpenaz, the master of the eunuchs, to bring back "...some of the children of Israel and some of the king's descendants and some of the nobles, young men in whom there was no blemish, but good-looking, gifted in all wisdom, possessing knowledge and quick to understand, who had ability to serve in the king's palace, and whom they might teach the language and literature of the Chaldeans" (Daniel 1:3-4).

In this far away place, Daniel would face new challenges and new temptations. His normal routine of life had been altered radically. He was now under the control of people who were not favorable to his God and his faith. He probably had many questions in his mind about what was ahead. Would he be able to practice his religion? What temptations lay ahead in this new place? Could he hold up under the pressure?

You know the story of Daniel and you know that it ends well for him. Daniel remained faithful throughout his days in Babylon, "... the king promoted Daniel and gave him many great gifts; and he made him ruler over the whole province of Babylon, and chief administrator over all the wise men of Babylon" (Daniel 2:48). He even found favor in the eyes of the kings that succeeded Nebuchadnezzar. "So this Daniel prospered in the reign of Darius and in the reign of Cyrus the Persian" (Daniel 6:28). What was it about Daniel that helped him maintain his faith in that distant land? He had developed good habits that he took with him when he was taken captive. Developing and maintaining good habits will help you keep the faith while you are away from home.

He had Good Physical Health Habits

The Jewish system included strict food laws. Leviticus 11 and 17 record God's regulations concerning clean and unclean animals and His prohibition against eating blood. Daniel's observance of these laws had been the habit of his life. "But Daniel purposed in his heart that he would not defile himself with the portion of the king's delicacies, nor with the wine which he drank; therefore he requested of the chief of the eunuchs that he might not defile himself" (Daniel 1:8).

However, this habit was challenged immediately, "...the king appointed for them a daily provision of the king's delicacies and of the wine which he drank, and three years of training for them, so that at the end of that time they might serve before the king." (Daniel 1:5) Daniel proposed a test, challenging the king's food with Daniel's food requirements from God. "Please test your servants for ten days, and let them give us vegetables to eat and water to drink. Then let our appearance be examined before you, and the appearance of the young men who eat the portion of the king's delicacies and as you see fit, so deal with your servants" (Daniel 1:12-13).

The result was just as Daniel had expected. "And at the end of ten days their features appeared better and fatter in flesh than all the young men who ate the portion of the king's delicacies" (Daniel 1:15). Only Daniel's resolve to stand firm on his convictions and his good health habit kept him from giving in to the king's food portions.

Good health habits are important. Paul reminded us, "...do you not know that your body is the temple of the Holy Spirit who is in you, whom you have from God, and you are not your own?" (I Corinthians 6:19) He followed this with this exhortation, "...glorify God in your body and in your spirit, which are God's" (I Corinthians 6:20). III John opens with an interesting statement about health. John wrote, "...I pray that you may prosper in all things and be in health, just as your soul prospers" (verse 2).

God is concerned about our health. There are a number of health passages in the Bible. "A merry heart does good like medicine..." (Proverbs 17:22). Part of your health should include laughing and enjoyment. Solomon recorded this advice to his son concerning health, "My son, give attention to my words; incline your ear to my sayings. Do not let them depart from your eyes; keep them in the midst of your heart; for they are life to those who find, and health to all their flesh" (Proverbs 4:20-22). The wise man taught his son that paying attention to wisdom from God reaps a healthy benefit to the body. Paul admitted to Timothy, "for bodily exercise profits a little…" (I Timothy 4:8). He went on, of course, to say that godliness profits a whole lot. But, he did acknowledge the health benefits of exercise.

Daniel's success away from home is, in part, due to his resolve to maintain the healthy habits he had been taught all of his life. These habits contributed to his being able to think clearly and be strong enough, physically, to face the temptations and challenges he confronted in that far away place.

He had Good Spiritual Health Habits

Daniel's greatest habits, of course, were his spiritual health habits. He was a spiritually-minded man who made sure that he held onto this part of his life, even in that far away land. These habits, combined with the physical health habits, made Daniel especially capable of thriving away from his home.

There are five spiritual habits that dominated Daniel's life. The first one is found in Daniel 2:19-23. King Nebuchadnezzar of Babylon was the ruler of the distant land where Daniel was living. One night, he had a dream and wanted to find its interpretation. He called in all of his wise men, commanding them to reveal the interpretation. In order to be sure of the truth of their interpretation, he also commanded them to tell him the dream as well. No wise man could even think of doing that. The resulting punishment of their failure was death!

Daniel contacted the king, volunteering to help the king and spare the wise men. Verse 19 says, "Then the secret was revealed to Daniel in a night vision. So Daniel blessed the God of Heaven." Before delivering the vision and its interpretation, Daniel paused to thank God for what he had done, (verses 20-23). Thankfulness to God is a necessary spiritual habit.

Later, in that same chapter, is a second spiritual habit of Daniel's. It becomes apparent as Daniel approaches the king to tell the vision. His first words honor God for the revelation, (verses 27-28). Daniel did not claim credit for himself. He was humble and wanted God to have the credit He deserved. You should give God the honor He deserves for what He has done in your life.

Daniel's greatest temptation came about because of another of his spiritual habits, (Daniel 6:1-28). Some men, who were jealous of the position and fame Daniel had gained in Babylon, used Daniel's habit of daily prayer to convince the king to throw him into the lion's den. They had tricked the king into signing an order that no one could pray to any god except the king for 30 days, under the penalty of the lion's den. They knew of Daniel's daily routine of prayer. They knew that he would pray anyway. Daniel's habit of prayer got him into trouble with some men of lower character, but it proved his spiritual strength.

Daniel's next two spiritual habits were connected with the previous one. Daniel 9 reveals that Daniel was a man of prayer who used prayer to confess his own sins, and those of his fellow countrymen, before God. He knew that his God was a God of forgiveness. He knew the importance of confessing sin and interceding on behalf of the sins of others. The willingness to confess your own sins is key for spiritual health.

While you are away from home, be sure to develop and maintain good habits. The physical habits are important, but don't just concentrate on them. The really important ones are the spiritual habits. They might be the harder ones to develop, but they are the most important.

Prayer: *Dear gracious Father, I give you thanks for all that you have done for me until this time. You are my God and I want to give You the honor that is due You. Please forgive me, for I admit that I am a sinner. I know that You forgive those who repent. I ask that You help me to develop the physical and spiritual habits that I need to remain faithful to You while I am away from home. In Jesus' name, Amen.*

Brainstorming Ideas to Make this a Reality in Your Life:

1. Make a list of things that you need to thank God for specifically and plan a time to do it.

2. The next time you assemble with the Saints for worship, remind yourself that this worship is to honor God.

3. Spend honest time with God in prayer about specific sins and weaknesses that you need help overcoming.

What other ideas do you have?
1.
2.
3.

Discussion Starters:

1. What things did Daniel have to be thankful to God for, seeing as he was captive in a distant land?

2. What are some ways that you can honor God in your daily life?

3. Why is it important to intercede before God on others' behalf?

4. How does physical health improve spiritual health?

While You Are Away From Home

CHAPTER 7
JACOB: WORK HARD

Read the Text: Genesis 25:12-33:20

Jacob and his brother had a rocky beginning. Even their births put them at odds with each other. Their mother had been barren and Isaac pleaded with the Lord to let her have a child. The Lord listened to him and gave them twins. "But the children struggled together within her and she said, 'If all is well, why am I like this?'" (Genesis 25:22). The Lord explained that the two were going to be heads of two nations and "...One people shall be stronger than the other, and the older shall serve the younger" (Genesis 25:23).

They became two very different individuals: "Esau was a skillful hunter, a man of the field; but Jacob was a mild man, dwelling in tents" (Genesis 25:27). And, "Isaac loved Esau because he ate of his game, but Rebekah loved Jacob" (Genesis 25:28). Eventually, Jacob tricked Esau into selling his birthright for a bowl of soup (Genesis 25:29-34). He later did the same thing to his father with his mother's help. Using his blindness against him, they tricked Isaac into believing that Jacob was Esau so Jacob could also get Esau's blessing, (Genesis 27:1-40). This drove Jacob away from home to his uncle, Laban, in Haran, (Genesis 27:41-28:5).

Jacob's lesson for us begins here. He had a chance meeting with Rachel, Laban's daughter, at a well near her home, (Genesis 29). Immediately, he was taken by her and determined to marry her. She led him and his traveling companions to her home where Laban greeted them warmly as family, giving him a place to stay; which Jacob did for about a month, (verse 14). Laban struck a deal with Jacob to work for him for 7 years to marry Rachel.

As you read the rest of the story of Jacob and his time with Laban, you will not appreciate everything that he did. However, you can appreciate and learn from his work ethic. It is an ethic that you should adopt while you are away from home.

Work Hard to Reach a Goal

Jacob made a deal to work for Laban for 7 years in order to achieve his goal, (Genesis 29:18). He was not discouraged by having to work. He did not expect to have his goal handed to him without paying a price. Neither the amount of time, nor the type of work, seemed to matter to him. Jacob's work ethic was solid and his resolve was true. He set out to do whatever he needed to do to be successful.

Whatever the reason or reasons for your being away from home, you will have to work hard to achieve your goals. No one is going to give you what you want. You will not be able to be lazy on your way through life and accomplish very much. There are many others out there who will be trying to achieve their goals, as well. You may have to compete to get ahead. You will have to sacrifice. You will have to exert yourself.

You may have heard the saying, "Hard work never hurt anyone!" It means that hard work will not make your life worse. The truth is that hard work will make you appreciate, even more, whatever you earn by working hard. There is no feeling quite like that of satisfaction at the end of a hard day's work. When you can look back at the day's work and see the positive results, it actually strengthens and encourages you. The reward of hard work is often the work itself and how it makes you a better person for having done it.

Furthermore, your future rewards of pay and advancement may very well depend on your hard work. Often, those who run businesses look out for those who work hard. They don't want to lose a hard worker to a competitor. Also, hard workers are usually the ones who get the promotions and advance upward through the chain of command. Work hard because hard work does not go unnoticed by those higher up.

Working Hard Makes Time Fly

Jacob was so dedicated and focused on his goal that the time passed by so much more quickly. The hard work kept him so busy that he really did not seem to notice the time. The text says, "So Jacob served seven years for Rachel, and they seemed only a few days to him because of the love he had for her" (Genesis 29:20).

If you are away from home because you are entering college, it may seem that you have a long journey ahead of you. You look down the road and see 4 years of college ahead, (unless you change your major or continue your education through a Master's program). Four years seems like a long time as you look ahead to it. However, graduation day will probably cause you to say, "I can't believe how fast it went by!"

If you are away from home because you are starting a job, you may feel that you have a long time ahead of you trying to advance to better jobs and better pay. It may, indeed, take some time for you to experience the success you want, but there will come a day when you will look back and think how fast the time has gone since you first entered the work force.

Hard work is one of the reasons for time moving by so fast. On the other hand, you may have experienced how tired you can be after a boring day of doing nothing. It seems that doing nothing all day and just lying around being lazy makes you more tired than exerting yourself all day to complete a task. It is an odd thing to think that working on a project is less tiring than doing nothing for an extended period of time.

Work Hard, Even When You are Mistreated

The story of Jacob is a story of mistreatment and deception. Jacob had fallen in love with Rachel, the younger daughter of Laban. After the 7 years had passed, Jacob came to Laban to ask for the right to marry Rachel, as he had been promised. Laban prepared the big wedding feast. "Now it came to pass in the evening, that he took Leah, his daughter, and brought her to Jacob; and he went in to her...So it came to pass in the morning, that behold, it was Leah. And he said to Laban, 'What is this you have done to me? Was it not for Rachel that I served you? Why then have you deceived me?" (Genesis 29:23, 25).

This is a little strange, based on our culture. However, in their culture it makes sense. The bride was completely covered during the wedding feast. Then, at night, the bride was taken to the home of the groom. Because it was dark, he could not see her face until the morning light. That is when he discovered he had been tricked and deceived! So, he had to work another 7 years in order to marry Rachel, (Genesis 29:26-27).

After 20 years, Jacob determined to leave Laban and return to his family. Because of the way he had been treated and deceived by Laban, Jacob ran away in the night. Three days later, Laban realized he had gone and pursued him. When he caught up to him, he accused Jacob of stealing from him and taking his daughters and grandchildren away without letting him say goodbye. Jacob responded to Laban's accusations,

"These twenty years I have been with you; your ewes and your female goats have not miscarried their young, and I have not eaten the rams of your flock. That which was torn by beasts I did not bring to you; I bore the loss of it. You required it from my hand, whether stolen by day or stolen by night. There I was! In the day the drought consumed me, and the frost by night, and my sleep departed from my eyes. Thus I have been in your house twenty years; I served you fourteen years for your two daughters, and six years for your flock, and you have changed my wages ten times" (Genesis 31:38-41).

You will not always be treated properly as an employee under an employer or as a student under a professor. That, however, does not give you the excuse to refuse to work hard. You will not appreciate yourself if you do not work hard, regardless of how you are treated. The only person you will be hurting is yourself if you do not work hard. The value of the hard work is worth whatever you have to endure while doing it. Remember: work hard for yourself. You are the one who will gain the most.

Prayer: *Dear Father in Heaven, praise be to your glorious name. Thank you for the opportunity to work hard and have success. I pray that You will help me to see the value of hard work by allowing me to have enough success to give me confidence. I pray, also, that You will give me enough difficulty so that I will need to rely on You and not on my own work. I pray, Father, that I will learn to work hard so that I will work hard for You as well. In the name of Jesus, I pray, Amen.*

Brainstorming Ideas to Make this a Reality in Your Life:

1. Tell yourself that you will not "just get by" in your work.

2. Do one more thing than is asked of you. Don't settle for the minimum work.

3. Take on a particular project that will require you to grow and stretch yourself.

4. Thank your parents for the work ethic they gave you.

What other ideas do you have?
1.
2.
3.

Discussion Starters:

1. What character traits are conducive to a good work ethic?

2. What character traits contribute to a poor work ethic?

3. What are some proper ways to respond when you are mistreated at work?

4. Why is a clear goal so important to one's work ethic?

CHAPTER 8
JESUS: STAY BUSY WITH THE RIGHT THINGS

Read the Text: Luke 2:51-52; Acts 10:38; John 9:4

You are on the verge of some of the most exciting times of your life! A whole new world will open up to you! You will make new friends and face new challenges. You will be responsible for yourself in ways you have not yet fully realized. You are on your own, ready to make your own decisions. Now, it is your life, more fully than ever before.

This could be the busiest time of your life. There will be no shortage of things to keep you occupied. The college environment is full of challenges to your time. Clubs and classes, friends and food, parties and people will all compete for your time. If you are away from home in the work environment, you, too, will be challenged to be busy. Your job will compete with your hobbies. Your boss will compete with your friends. Your biggest challenge will not be to stay busy. It will be to stay busy with the right things.

Jesus provides us a great example of staying busy with the right things while He was away from home. He left the portals of His heavenly home to come to this earth. He knew at an early age that He was here to be busy. He told His parents, who had been looking for Him when He stayed behind after their time at the Feast of the Passover, "Why do you seek Me? Did you not know that I must be about My Father's business?" (Luke 2:49). His whole life was dedicated to staying busy doing what He was called to do. From His life, we learn about staying busy.

The Right Things Should be Your Business

Following the incident at the Feast of the Passover when He was 12, the Bible tells us, "Then He went down with them (His parents) and came to Nazareth, and was subject to them..." (Luke 2:51). This is significant because Jesus was busy in the right way, learning the right things to provide us the right lessons how to be busy in the right way ourselves. From Luke 2:52, we learn that Jesus was busy learning the right things.

51

"And Jesus increased in wisdom and stature, and in favor with God and men." The right things were His business and the same right things should be your business.

While you are away from home, it is right to stay busy maturing in wisdom. Wisdom will come from the situations you encounter. Gain all the proper knowledge you can get. It will serve you well as you make decisions that will affect your life in the present and in the future.

While you are away from home, it is right to stay busy maturing in stature. It is important for you to be concerned about your physical strength and growth. Develop good habits of exercise and diet. These will serve you well the rest of your life. Very often, your habits of exercise and diet now will be a factor in your future health.

While you are away from home, it is right to stay busy maturing spiritually. This is not the time to sow wild oats - there never is a proper time for this! Continue your well-established habits of spiritual growth. Assembling with the saints on a regular basis should be a staple part of your spiritual diet. Personal Bible study and prayer are also very important. Develop Christian friends who will give you encouragement and help.

While you are away from home, it is right to stay busy maturing socially. You will come into contact with many different people. Some of them will be good for your development, while others will not. But, it is good for you to develop good social connections. No one can make it in this life alone. Some of the friends you make during this time will be with you for the rest of your life. Make sure that you develop healthy relationships in your life. This is really important in your dating relationships. Don't allow yourself to be abused or mistreated.

Your Reputation will Come from the Things that Keep You Busy

If you were asked to summarize the life of Jesus in just a few words, what would you say? When Luke wrote his two-volume set—Luke/Acts—he detailed the life of Jesus in Luke and he detailed the beginnings of the Church in Acts. He was writing to a man named Theophilus in order that he might "know the certainty of those things in which you were instructed" (Luke 1:4).

He had, apparently, been taught about Jesus and needed a final summary of assurance. Luke wrote a clear, brief, to-the-point summary of the life of Jesus in Acts 10:38 when he wrote, "…God anointed Jesus of Nazareth with the Holy Spirit and with power, who went about doing good and healing all who were oppressed by the devil, for God was with Him." This is a great summary of the life Jesus! This is His reputation!

There are two points to Jesus' reputation. First, He went about doing good. Jesus spent His life helping others and teaching others. His reputation was so wide-spread during His years of ministry that multitudes of people followed Him around constantly. Matthew's gospel mentions the multitudes of people 38 times. One of those passages, Matthew 4:25 reads, "Great multitudes followed Him—from Galilee, and from Decapolis, Jerusalem, Judea, and beyond the Jordan." The multitudes followed Jesus because He did good all of the time.

The second part of Jesus' reputation that Luke mentions is, "for God was with Him". His reputation came from His actions around the people, but it also came from His obvious connection with God. Everyone knew God was with Him, even if they did not want to believe it. One man expressed those sentiments in John 3:2, "Rabbi, we know that You are a teacher come from God; for no one can do these signs that You do unless God is with him." This man was Nicodemus. He was a ruler of the Jews and a Pharisee. He merely expressed the obvious truth that everyone seemed to recognize.

While you are away from home, your reputation will be very important. Christians have the responsibility to follow the example that Jesus has set before us. "For to this you were called, because Christ also suffered for us, leaving us an example, that you should follow His steps…" (I Peter 2:21-25).

Stay busy developing the reputation of doing good, (and of being good), while you are on your own away from home. There will be many people who will tempt you to do what they are doing and to be a part of their activities. Some of them will not be activities that a Christian should participate in. Determine to be good and to do good. Fight the temptation to "fit in" at any cost.

The more you are successful establishing your good habits, the more you will be seen in the same way that Jesus was. Everyone should be able to say of a Christian that God is with them. Christians should live in such a way that others give God the glory for what they see in them, (Matthew 5:16). As God was with Jesus and others saw it, you should live in such a way that others will see God living in and through you.

The Time to be Busy is Now

Unfortunately, there are many who leave home and decide to use that time to do their own thing. It is not that they have made a decision to leave the Lord behind forever. They just want to spend a little time away from Him so that they can be free of the burden of living up to a standard that keeps them from doing the fun things that everyone else seems to be doing. They want their own space in their own place. That pretty well summarizes the attitude of many while they are away from home.

Jesus not only recognized that He needed to stay busy doing the right things, He also knew the importance of staying busy doing the right things *now*. He said to His disciples, "I must work the works of Him who sent Me while it is day; the night is coming when no one can work" (John 9:4).

Jesus acknowledged a fact that you need to see, as well. There will come a time when you will no longer be able to be busy for the Lord. You will not live forever on this earth. The day of your death will come someday. It could come for any one person at any time. It is important, therefore, to be busy now pursuing the proper things. If you pursue the proper things now, you will be ready whenever your time on this earth ends.

The most important principle for your life is for you to live as a Christian. Your parents want you to put God first above everything else. Your Christian friends want you to live as a faithful Christian so that you can be an encouragement to them. And, you want to live as a Christian as well. Don't let yourself, your friends, your parents, and your God down by misusing your time away from home.

No good thing can come from putting your Christian life on hold while you pursue your own desires first. The night may come when you either don't want to come back and do right or don't have the opportunity to come back because you meet the time of your death unprepared for the next life.

While you are away from home, stay busy with the right things so that you will have a reputation that pleases your parents and honors your God. Stay busy doing the right things *now*. Don't put them on hold for a later time. The very best time is now. It is the only time that you are guaranteed to have!

Prayer: *Gracious God and Father of all, You have been so good to me all my life. You have given me a wonderful family and wonderful friends who have taught me about You. Help me to be faithful to You while I am away from them. Give me opportunities to do good for other people. And, may the good that I have the chance to do give glory to Your great Name! In the name of Your Son who showed me how to live doing good and then died for me, Amen.*

Brainstorming Ideas to Make this a Reality in Your Life:

1. Before you get to the place where you will be away from home, find the Lord's Church and contact them to let them know that you will be in their town.

2. Find ways to volunteer where you are.

3. Ask to be involved with Church while you are there.

4. Thank your parents for showing you what is right.

What other ideas do you have?
1.
2.
3.
4.

Discussion Starters:

1. What are the dangers that confront a Christian who does not stay busy with the Lord?

2. Why should you stay busy with your Christian life and not take time off to "sow your wild oats"?

3. What traits of busy people do you admire?

4. Look up Bible passages about work and develop a picture of what God says about the topic.

While You Are Away From Home

CHAPTER 9
GOOD SAMARITAN: DON'T BE SO FOCUSED ON SELF THAT YOU IGNORE SOMEONE IN NEED

Read the text: Luke 10:25-37

Jesus told a story, in Luke 10, about a man whom we have come to identify as the good Samaritan. He was away from home in more ways than one. He was away from home because he was on a journey, (v. 33). But, he was also away from home because he was in a foreign country. The events of the story take place on the road between Jerusalem and Jericho. This is in the country of Judea.

A man was traveling this road when he was overtaken by thieves, beaten, robbed, and left to die. There were three men who encountered his situation. The first two were religious leaders. It would seem that they would have been the first to help, but they passed him by, instead. The one who helped was the one no one would have expected.

The Samaritan was in the land of people who did not like him. The Jews hated the Samaritans because they were half-breed Jews. Their hatred went way back to the years following the Assyrian captivity of Israel, around 722 BC. The poor Jews who were left in the land when the Assyrians took the rest of their countrymen into captivity intermarried with the Gentile population that moved into the mostly-vacant land. These marriages produced a mixed race of people who were neither fully Jews, nor fully Gentiles. The Jewish community did not accept them.

Not only did the Samaritan encounter this situation in a foreign land of people who did not like him, but the one who was in need was, himself, a Jew! No one would have blamed him if he had walked away. He was in a dangerous situation. He was among people who hated his very presence. Why should he stop and help? Shouldn't he just get back home to his own people?

This man helped another in need because he was not so focused on himself that he overlooked the opportunity to help someone in need.

There were many concerns that he might have concentrated on instead of thinking about the man in need.

There were racial concerns that could have consumed him. He was a hated man, merely because of his ancestors. He had not done anything, personally, to any Jew, yet most everyone in the area was against him.

There were financial concerns. He was away from home. He needed enough money to get home. Furthermore, how could he be expected to use his money to help someone who probably despised him, anyway?

And, what about possible risks to his own life? The area was, obviously, a dangerous one. Maybe those who had harmed the man on the side of the road were still in the area. Maybe he should just slink away. Someone else, surely, would come along and help the man.

Finally, the Samaritan might have reasoned, "Forget about getting a 'thank you'. I will never get one from this Jew!" Probably no one would have thought any different. It's not easy to help someone who does not appreciate it. But, this good man was thinking about the man in need, not of his own needs if he were to help.

So, why did the religious men not help the injured man? They may have thought that their job was more important than stopping to help. If they were to stop, they might be late to perform their duties at the temple. Their failure to help signaled to others that their religion was all talk and no action.

They may have thought that they were more important than the man in need. Maybe they reasoned that stooping to help him was, somehow, beneath them. He was beneath them, but not because they were so much better. They were just unwilling to bend.

Or, maybe they were so focused on the letter of the law that they overlooked the spirit. This man in need would have made them unclean if they had stopped to help. They would not have been able to perform their service at the temple without going through a period of cleansing. In truth, however, their failure to help made them unclean in the eyes of the God who wrote, in the letter of the law, "You shall love your neighbor as yourself" (Matthew 22:39; Leviticus 19:18).

While you are away from home pursuing your goals and aspirations, you will be focused on yourself and that is understandable. You have a job to do; you are pursuing an education, if you are in college or you have been hired to do a job. You must meet the demands of your particular situation. Do not fail in this.

However, may it never be that you get to be so focused on yourself that you fail to see those around you who are in need. Sure, helping someone will take an investment of time, energy, and resources. But, it will make you a better person. It will give you the opportunity to practice the words of Jesus that men have come to call "The Golden Rule": "Therefore, whatever you want men to do to you, do also to them, for this is the Law and the Prophets" (Matthew 7:12).

There will be challenges that you will need to confront. There will be the challenge of time. From time to time, we all feel that we do not have enough time to do what we want and need. But, we all have the same amount of time. Some fill that time wisely while others fill it haphazardly and poorly. But, we have more control over time than we are usually willing to admit. The thief of time is our own selfish desires and, maybe, a little laziness. Use your time wisely and you will find that you do have time to help others in need.

You might, also, face the challenge of people who do not like you. No one is liked by everyone. We all have those who do not like us and whom we do not like. However, this should never be an issue used to determine whether we will help someone in need. The Bible teaches that "while we were still sinners, Christ died for us" (Romans 5:8). Jesus died for people who did not like Him and even for those who actually put Him to death! Surely, we can help someone today who may not like us very much! After all, they have not tried to kill us. But, even if they did...

There is also the challenge of resources. College students and those who have just entered the workforce probably do not have the financial means to help everyone. That is no reason, however, not to help someone. If you can buy a pizza whenever you want, you have some money that you can use to help someone if they really need it.

But, money is not the only resource available to you. In addition to your time, there is the resource of your talents. Each one of us has talents and abilities that can be very valuable to someone in need. If you can jump someone's car that won't start, if you can fix a computer that has locked up, or if you change a car tire, you have a resource that will come in handy for someone at sometime. Just keep your eyes and ears open.

So, why should a Christian help someone in need? That's what Christians do. Christians should be like Christ. Acts 10:38 states that He "went about doing good." Furthermore, we are supposed to follow the example that He has left for us (I Peter 2:21). We cannot claim to be

Christ's if we refuse to help others as we can.

Finally, Christians should help others because our actions are very important in helping others come to understand and appreciate God. Jesus stated it this way in a very familiar passage, "Let your light so shine before men that they may see your good works and glorify your Father who is in heaven" (Matthew 5:16). While you are away from home, be sure that you do not stay so busy with your own life that you fail to see and help others who are in need. That is the essence of Christianity.

Prayer: *Gracious Father, open my eyes to the needs of others in life. Help me not to dwell so much on my own life that the lives of others go unnoticed. Use me often to show Jesus to someone in need and, in so doing, be reminded that I am continually in need of Your grace and mercy. Remind me that only by helping others can I expect to be helped. I don't want to be selfish. I want to share with others what You have shared with me—the greatest help of all, Your Son for my sins. Thank you for that help. In His name, Amen.*

Brainstorming Ideas to Make this a Reality in Your Life:

1. Get involved in a service project for someone less fortunate than yourself.

2. Visit a nursing home, retirement center, or hospital.

3. Thank your parents for helping you learn to care about other people.

What other ideas do you have?
1.
2.
3.

Discussion Starters:

1. Why does helping someone else seem to help you even more?

2. What attitudes are necessary to have to be able to help someone whom you do not like, or may even be an enemy?

3. What are some ways that all college students or young people can help others?

While You Are Away From Home

CHAPTER 10
AQUILA AND PRISCILLA: DON'T RUN FROM A CHANCE TO TEACH SOMEONE

Read the Text Acts 18:1-28

Aquila and Priscilla were in Corinth when Paul met them, (Acts 18:1-17). They had previously been in Rome, however, Claudius Caesar had decreed that all Jews were to leave the city. They were forced from their home and set up their lives as tentmakers in Corinth. Paul was of the same occupation, so he worked with them during his time there. They must have formed a great friendship and working relationship because when Paul sailed for Syria, Aquila and Priscilla went with him. These two took up residence in Ephesus when Paul sailed on to Jerusalem, (Acts 18:18-20).

This was their second move away from home. They could have been angry because of the decree that forced them away. They could have worked actively against the government of the day. They even could have reacted in the way many others have, becoming angry with God for allowing such things to happen to them after they had devoted their lives to serving Him.

But, Aquila and Priscilla displayed a true Christian nature and evangelistic focus. Their moves to Corinth and Ephesus put them in positions to serve God through teaching the gospel to any who would listen. They worked diligently alongside Paul in Corinth, where the following results are recorded, "Then Crispus, the ruler of the synagogue, believed on the Lord with all his household. And many of the Corinthians, hearing, believed and were baptized" (Acts 18:8).

In Ephesus, they heard Apollos, a Jewish convert from John the baptizer's teaching, preaching in the city the only thing that he knew—John's baptism (Acts 18:24-25). Aquila and Priscilla were not ones to hold back when something needed to be corrected in the presentation of the gospel. So, they called him aside "…and explained to him the way of God more accurately" (Acts 18:26). Not only did they teach him the truth more perfectly, they led the Christians of Ephesus to contact the brethren of Achaia to let them know that he was now teaching the truth in its fullness. The effect of their initiative was apparent immediately; "...and when he arrived, he greatly helped those who had believed through grace; for he vigorously refuted the Jews publicly, showing from the Scriptures that Jesus is the Christ" (Acts 18:28).

Aquila and Priscilla set a prime example of taking with them their responsibility as Christians to preach the gospel. Even though they might not have been as comfortable as they would have been at home, even the though the surroundings might not have been very familiar, and even though they were not with their Christian support group back home, nevertheless, they did not run from an opportunity to teach the gospel to someone along the way. So, what have they taught us about following their example?

Don't Make Excuses for Not Sharing Jesus

We are all pretty good at making excuses for things that we don't want to do or that we are not as comfortable doing, but there are no excuses for failing to share Jesus. That is what Christianity is all about. There will be no Christians in Heaven who have never tried to share Jesus with others who do not know Him. Both passively, through proper living, and actively, approaching someone in some way with the Good News, Christians have a responsibility to share the message of the gospel.

Scripture is clear on this matter. Peter encouraged, "But sanctify the Lord God in your hearts, and always be ready to give a defense to everyone who asks you a reason for the hope that is in you, with meekness and fear..." (I Peter 3:15). There will be people who will approach us asking for our help to know Jesus. Be ready!

Jesus stated, "Let your light so shine before men, that they may see your good works and glorify your Father in Heaven" (Matthew 5:16). He told His disciples that they were "the salt of the earth" (Matthew 5:13) and "the light of the world" (Matthew 5:14). Living the Christian example as a disciple of Jesus is the way to call attention to the God we serve. This is the most basic way of showing others about Jesus—spreading the Word with our lives. Be consistent!

Jesus' words in Mark 16:15 give His disciples a clear marching order. "Go into all the world and preach the gospel to every creature." All disciples of Jesus will seek out ways that they can spread the Word wherever they are, whether it be passing out study materials, or studying with someone across a table, or setting up the opportunity for someone else to study with them.

Aquila and Priscilla could have used all kinds of excuses not to be

While You Are Away From Home

evangelistic. Let us notice some potential excuses they encountered that also confront us today. Remember, they were away from home just like you, yet they did not offer any of these excuses.

Don't Make the Excuse that You are Too Small to Do This

Aquila and Priscilla were not professional teachers. They were simple tent-makers. This was a trade (Acts 18:3). In other words, they were not schooled in the world of academia to learn this trade. Maybe, they had gone to some kind of technical school or maybe they had learned this work as apprentices under someone else. In either case, this was not a glamorous job. It certainly required skill; it was hard work making these tents sewing every stitch by hand. However, the tent-maker was not high on the social ladder of the day.

These two disciples did not look at their place in life and decide that they were too small to approach anyone who needed to hear the gospel. They were not self-absorbed; they were selfless. They were not focused on their place in the social circles. They were focused on their place in the *spiritual* circles.

Sharing the gospel does not require any special talent or standing; neither do you have to be able to quote the Bible or the major portion of it. The only prerequisite is that you be a Christian, yourself. Then, all you have to do is share with someone what you learned and did in order to be right with the Lord. Remember this: as a Christian you stand in the highest social class possible. You are a child of God! His family is your family. There is no need to think that you are not good enough to share with others what you have done!

Don't Make the Excuse that Someone is Too Big for You to Approach With the Gospel

Apollos is described as "an eloquent man and mighty in the Scriptures" (Acts 18:24). Furthermore, "this man had been instructed in the way of the Lord; and being fervent in spirit..." (Acts 18:25). He was educated, eloquent, and enthusiastic. He was a "big" name. He had been preaching for a while, it seems. He might have been a very imposing character.

But, he was just a man. At least, that must have been what Aquila and Priscilla saw. He was a capable speaker, but he did not speak the full truth. He was full of what he believed and preached; he just did not have the full gospel. The only recourse that Aquila and Priscilla thought they had was to approach him and help him learn the truth. He was not imposing to them for they were not looking at him - they were looking at what he was saying.

There are no people who are so big that they do not need to hear the truth of the Gospel. It is also not true that just because someone is "bigger" than you that you stand no chance of influencing them for the Lord. There are many who have been won to the Lord by someone less educated and less talented.

Don't Make the Excuse That you Won't Make a Real Difference

Just what did Aquila and Priscilla hope to accomplish when they approached Apollos? There can be only one answer to that question and it has nothing to do with the response of Apollos. They had no control over his response. The only difference they could make in the situation was sharing the Truth with someone who did not know it.

They could have reasoned that his education and expertise were evidences that they would not be able to make any difference in the situation. However, they knew they could make one difference. They knew they could share with him the complete truth of the gospel. That is a big difference! Before they talked with him, he did not know the complete truth. After they talked with him, he knew the complete truth.

There will be opportunities for you to share the Gospel with someone who already has education and expertise in the Bible, however, they don't have the complete truth. The difference you can make is to give them the complete truth. Don't forget this very important point. The power that can change someone is not in you; it is in the truth of the Gospel (Romans 1:16).

This point is discussed more fully in I Corinthians 3:5-8. Paul says, "Who then is Paul, and who is Apollos, but ministers through whom you believed, as the Lord gave to each one? I planted, Apollos watered, but God gave the increase." The two verses show our proper place in the presentation of the truth. It is our job to share the truth. God takes care of the increase.

Furthermore, he says, "So then neither he who plants is anything, nor he who waters, but God who gives the increase. Now he who plants and he who waters are one, and each one will receive his own reward according to his own labor." Paul tells us to pay attention only to the thing that we can control and in which we can make a difference—spreading the Word. We cannot control whether or not someone accepts the truth. We are called to make an informational difference in others' lives. They are, then, called to make a transformational difference in their own lives.

While you are away from home, be evangelistic. Don't run from opportunities to share the message of God's Word. I know that you are happy that someone did not run from the opportunity to share the message with you.

Prayer: *Dear Father in Heaven, thank You for the Word that You have left with us so that we might know. Thank you, specifically, that someone shared that Word with me. Now, I ask that You give me opportunities to share Jesus with others, strength to meet the challenge, and courage to do it. Help me to rely on Your promise to increase the Word sown. Help me to be a sower of the Word. In Jesus' name, Amen.*

Brainstorming Ideas to Make this a Reality in Your Life:

1. Find a tract or lesson that you can hand out to friends.

2. Invite someone to worship.

3. Take a Bible study course and invite a friend to take it with you.

What other ideas do you have?
1.
2.
3.

Discussion Starters:

1. Why is it so hard to approach others about their relationship with Jesus?

2. What things would help you be more courageous to share Jesus with your friends?

3. Why do you think others are hesitant to study the Bible and learn about Jesus?

While You Are Away From Home

CHAPTER 11
SHADRACH, MESHACH, ABEDNEGO: STAND BY YOUR CONVICTIONS

Read the text: Daniel 1:1-21; 3:1-30

Going away from home for the first time can be a very scary experience. You are not the only one to have some hesitation, even though you are also excited about the new adventures. Your going away from home is not scary only for you; your parents are nervous, too! If you are the first one to leave the nest, their concern is justified. They wonder if they have taught you enough to be able to do well without their constant attention. If you are not the first, then the known concerns of your siblings who preceded your leaving are added to their concerns for you. It seems like an impossible situation for both of you!

However, the most important part of your time away from home, and the part that causes the most concern for parents and those who love you, is not you. They are concerned about everyone you will encounter as you leave home. They know about temptations and challenges you will face. They know how difficult it will be to face them successfully every time. They want you to be strong and face whatever comes your way with conviction. All who care about you want you to hold onto the convictions they have helped to form in you.

Your Convictions Will be Challenged

Shadrach, Meshach, and Abed-Nego did not choose to leave home. They were taken into captivity in Babylon, (Daniel 1:1-4). They were forced to leave their homes, but they still faced the same challenge that you will face: they had to hold onto their convictions against whatever was going to challenge them. And, they were challenged!

Just five verses into their story in the book of Daniel, we read of the first challenge these three friends faced in that far away place. It was an indirect assault on their personal convictions. The king determined that he would prepare certain of the captive men to serve in his kingdom. "Then the king instructed Ashpenaz, the master of his eunuchs, to bring some of the children of Israel and some of the king's descendants and some of the nobles, young men in whom there was no blemish, but good-looking, gifted in all wisdom, possessing knowledge and quick to understand, who had ability to serve in the king's palace, and whom they might teach the language and literature of the Chaldeans" (Daniel 1:3-4).

Though this might be distasteful to these Jewish boys, it was not something that would have been sinful for them to do. That is, it would not be sinful for them if they could retain their standing faithfully to their Jewish convictions. And, that was the problem. The very first order was a challenge to their convictions about eating. "And the king appointed for them a daily provision of the king's delicacies and of the wine which he drank…" (Daniel 1:5). These orders were for the purpose of making them as healthy as the people of that time thought they could be.

Their second great test was much more terrifying, (Daniel 3:1-30). This challenge was a direct assault on the God of the universe and whether they would stand with Him or with the king and all the others who gave in to the king.

King Nebuchadnezzar was an arrogant man. He seemed to be highly enamored with himself. He would later pay a great price for this character flaw, (Daniel 4). On this occasion he decided to honor himself with an image of gold that stood 90 feet tall and 9 feet wide! He set it up in the plain of Dura, probably so that more people could see it. Then, he demanded that everyone fall down and worship it when the trumpet sounded.

Shadrach, Meshach, and Abed-Nego refused to bow as everyone around them did. They knew the penalty for this refusal. "…at the time you hear the sound of the horn, flute, harp, lyre, and psaltery, in symphony with all kinds of music, and you fall down and worship the image which I have made, good! But if you do not worship, you shall be cast immediately into the midst of a burning fiery furnace" (Daniel 3:15). So, what can you learn about the challenge of convictions from these young men?

Know the Convictions You Will Stand For

These young men had already decided what their answers would be when their convictions would be challenged. Their convictions were theirs, they did not belong to their parents! They understood well a very basic principle: decide what you believe before you are tested. If you wait until you are challenged to decide, you will make more wrong decisions than right ones. It is not easy in the heat of a moment to decide what you believe about whatever the challenge is.

It is, also, important that you understand another basic principle: you better stand for something or you will fall for everything. This means that if you do not have some foundational beliefs—uncompromisables—you can be persuaded more easily away from the right pathway. Uncompromisables are those core things that you are not willing to change for anyone—parents, spouse, or best friend. They are the core beliefs that define who you are spiritually.

There is a final principle you can learn from the actions of these young men. You cannot pick and choose the parts of things you stand for; it's all or nothing. These friends knew they could not stand for the dress regulations, the feast regulations, or the sacrifice regulations and overlook the food regulations and the worship regulations and still be true to their convictions. This was a package deal. It was the entire law of Moses for the Jews, or none of it was worth standing up for. Today, you cannot pick and choose what you will stand for in the New Testament. It, too, is an all-or-nothing proposition.

Stand Up for Your Convictions, Even If You Stand Alone

The text of Daniel does not indicate how many young men were a part of the leadership building plans of King Nebuchadnezzar. Neither is there a record of how many people were on hand when the music signaled that they were supposed to bow down and worship. However, the record is very clear about the actions of Shadrach, Meshach, and Abed-Nego.

To the king's demand that they eat a certain diet, they proposed a different test. They proposed to be allowed to eat and drink after the laws of their Jewish faith and be compared to the others who were eating the king's diet. The proposition was accepted and, of course, they stood far above the rest, (Daniel 1:8-21).

To the king's challenge to bow down and worship or be thrown into a burning furnace of fire, they boldly answered, "O Nebuchadnezzar, we have no need to answer you in this matter. If that is the case, our God whom we serve is able to deliver us from the burning fiery furnace, and He will deliver us from your hand, O king. But if not, let it be known to you, O king, that we do not serve your gods, nor will we worship the gold image which you have set up" (Daniel 3:16-18).

In such challenges, these friends showed the strength of their convictions. From them you should learn three things:

1. What is popular is not always right.
2. What is right is not always popular.
3. God will honor your choice to stand by your convictions. Remember the words of Matthew 10:32-33, " Therefore whoever confesses Me before men, him I will also confess before My Father, who is in Heaven. But whoever denies Me before men, him I will also deny before My Father, who is in Heaven."

When You Stand, the Heat Will Rise

Shadrach, Meshach, and Abed-Nego knew what they were going to do, no matter the personal cost. Therefore, it should not have surprised them when some of the Chaldeans were watching them to see what they would do with the order to worship the idol, (Daniel 3:8). It appears they might have been a bit jealous of the position into which the king had placed them. They said to the king, "There are certain Jews whom you have set over the affairs of the province..." (Daniel 3:12).

Furthermore, they appealed to the vanity of the king. "...these men, O king, have not paid due regard to you. They do not serve your gods or worship the gold image which you have set up" (Daniel 3:12). This turned up the heat in the heart of King Nebuchadnezzar, as he flew into a "rage and fury", (Daniel 3:13) commanding the men to be brought to him. He assured them that if they did not do as he decreed he would really turn up the heat, literally; "He spoke and commanded that they heat the furnace seven times more than it was usually heated" (Daniel 3:19).

These young men were not hurting anyone by their refusal to fall before the image. The only one taking a beating was the ego of a king. You will feel the heat increasing against you as you live and act in ways that reveal others' low character and your high convictions. But remember, as these three men did, that you will feel the heat, but it can never destroy you eternally. "And do not fear those who kill the body, but cannot kill the soul. But, rather, fear Him who is able to destroy both soul and body in Hell" (Matthew 10:28).

You Never Really Stand Alone

The most important lesson to be learned from the courage of these men comes from the middle of the fiery furnace. They ended up right where they knew they would and they knew who would be right there with them. They might not have figured that their help actually would have been in the fire with them, but He was. "Then King Nebuchadnezzar was astonished; and he rose in haste and spoke, saying to his counselors, 'Did we not cast three men bound into the midst of the fire?...I see four men loose, walking in the midst of the fire; and they are not hurt, and the form of the fourth is like the Son of God" (Daniel 3:24-25).

The faith they had in their God, combined with the courage of their convictions to stand against the heat of the moment, was very influential. Shadrach, Meshach, and Abed-Nego had won a convert through their actions. They knew their convictions and stood on them, even if it meant standing alone and being persecuted or, even killed for them because they knew they were never alone.

The king was moved. He declared, "Blessed be the God of Shadrach, Meshach, and Abed-Nego, who sent His Angel and delivered His servants who trusted in Him, and they have frustrated the king's word, and yielded their bodies, that they should not serve nor worship any god except their own God! Therefore I make a decree that any people, nation, or language which speaks anything amiss against the God of Shadrach, Meshach, and Abed-Nego shall be cut in pieces, and their houses shall be made an ash heap; because there is no other God who can deliver like this" (Daniel 3:28-29).

While you are away from home, stand by your convictions. Not only will you be stronger yourself, you could also have a part in changing the lives of others who are influenced by the strength of your convictions.

Prayer: *Dear Father, I want to give You praise as the God of Heaven and Earth. I know that there is no other God but You. You deserve all the glory and honor. I pray that You will help me to stand strong against those who try to challenge my convictions. Help me to hold fast to what is right and help me to be willing to change any convictions that I learn not to be right. I pray for courage to endure those times when my convictions are challenged, knowing that only in the heat of testing can I know that they are of value. In the name of Jesus, Amen.*

Brainstorming Ideas to Make this a Reality in Your Life:

1. Make a list of your most basic convictions; put them to the test, through God's Word and through wise counsel.

2. Discuss your convictions with someone who holds a different one.

3. Thank your parents for the convictions they have given you.

What other ideas do you have?
1.
2.
3.

Discussion Starters:

1. How do you define the word "convictions"?

2. Why do people challenge your convictions? Why are they so intent on watching you fail?

3. Why is standing up for your convictions so important?

4. Where do convictions come from?

5. How does God stand with us today?

CHAPTER 12
JOHN THE BAPTIZER: FULFILL WHAT IS EXPECTED OF YOU

Read the text: Matthew 3:1-17; Mark 1:1-11; Luke 1:1-25, 57-80; John 1:6-13, 19-34; 3:1-22

As you leave home, you do so full of expectations. It is an exciting time. It is a time to stretch and to grow. It seems like the whole world has been opened up to you in a way that you have never experienced before. You now expect to be able to live your life the way that you want to live it, away from the gazing eyes of family and friends. It is your time to shine and you can hardly wait to get started!

One of the keys to living a satisfying life is to fulfill certain expectations that you take with you into this new existence. These expectations have come to you from different sources and you need to understand them, appreciate them, and handle them properly. For this study, we will consider the example of John the baptizer. He certainly had a lot of expectations laid on him from various places! From his success, you can learn how to fulfill your expectations.

Fulfill the Expectations You Have of Yourself

You have probably been thinking for a long time about the time that you get to leave home. It's not that you no longer enjoy being home; it is simply part of a normal maturation process. You are ready to strike out on your own and find your own way. It, also, does not mean that you are fully confident about leaving. But, it is true that the desire to go outweighs the desire to stay.

So, what do you expect of yourself as you go away? All people have expectations of themselves as they leave. Some are more mature than others, but we all have them. Have you thought about what you will major in, if you are going off to college? Have you thought about how you will spend your money, if you are going off to work? What recreational activities do you intend to pursue? Have you found the Lord's Church where you are going?

John the baptizer knew what to expect of himself in the work to which he was going. He knew that he would spend his time in the wilderness preaching the kingdom of God. Therefore, Luke 1:80 reads, "So the child grew and became strong in spirit, and was in the deserts till the day of his manifestation to Israel." John prepared himself for his work by being in the place where he would do his work. He was living true to the expectations he had of himself if he was going to fulfill the job that had been given to him.

I hope you know what to expect of yourself while you are away from home. Your expectations of yourself should be based on the talents you possess, the things that interest you, and, most importantly, the convictions of your faith. Give some thought to specific expectations, even taking the time to write them down. Be accountable to yourself. Call others into your accountability circle to help you, if you need them.

The expectations you have of yourself should be high enough to challenge you, but not so high as to discourage you. Someone has said, "Shoot for the moon. If you miss, you will still be among the stars." Don't be satisfied simply to float along, settling for whatever is easier or quicker. Expect that you will set a course and habit of life that will give you fulfillment as you fulfill what you expect of yourself.

Fulfill the Expectations Others Have of You

John the baptizer based his expectations of himself on the expectations he knew God had of him. Matthew records the words of the prophet Isaiah when he said, referring to John, "The voice of one crying in the wilderness; prepare the way of the LORD; make His paths straight" (Matthew 3:3). John's mission was laid out by God! Maybe you are thinking, "Well, John had no choice. He knew what he was supposed to do and just set out to do it. I don't have a clue what I want to do in my life. I wish God would just lay out my life for me, like He did for John!"

But, John did not lose his free will just because God prophesied about his mission. He had to choose to be faithful and accomplish what God intended. Furthermore, it is not as though he had been given a cushy job to do. He was going to be in the wilderness away from people and in a harsh environment. He wore camel hair clothes, (and camel's hair is not soft like wool), and ate locusts and wild honey. He gladly took on the trappings of the job to which he had been called because God called him to it.

You, too, have been called to a job by God. He has not prophesied anything about you as detailed as He did about John, but that does not mean that He has not revealed His expectations for you. While you are away from home, you are still under obligation to live a faithful life, putting God first in all you do, (Matthew 22:37). Make sure that what God expects of you is the highest of the expectations that you fulfill.

Your parents, also, have some expectations of you. They have probably communicated them to you in some way. It likely has something to do with grades in college, honesty in the workplace, and faithfulness in life. You might be able to tell a story of a time that your parents, one or both, sat you down and told you something specific they expected as you go away from home. Whatever the specifics are, honor those expectations. Your parents have only your best interests at heart. Zacharias, John's father, told his expectations of his son in Luke 1:76-79. What an awesome mission he knew his son had before him! Your parents know that you, too, have an awesome mission to "Let your light so shine before men, that they may see your good works and glorify your Father, who is in Heaven" (Matthew 5:16).

Even your friends and those who support you will have expectations of you. Their expectations of you will be based on who they understand you to be. They will respond to your actions and expect certain things because of how you live. There were many who supported John in his work and expected the help that he could offer them. Matthew 3:5-6 records that "Jerusalem and all Judea, and all the region around the Jordan went out to him and were baptized by him in the Jordan, confessing their sins." Because of his preaching, they expected certain things of him and he fulfilled every one of them.

As you fulfill the expectations that others have of you, be warned that you cannot make everyone happy all of the time. You may have many people come to you expecting things of you and vying for your time and energy. You need to be a giving person and help as many people as you can, but you cannot satisfy everyone who will expect something of you. Some of their expectations will be unreasonable. Others will be insulting. Still, others, might even be criminal. You cannot subject yourself to the whims and desires of everyone merely to make them happy. Some people will be unhappy because of some of your decisions, but that is to be expected.

The danger in meeting the expectations of others is two-fold. You might be tempted to lower your expectations to make others, and even yourself, happy. Many Christian young people have lowered their convictions simply to fit into the environment that they have chosen for themselves away from home. Others have studied less, partied more, and, generally, lowered themselves to the standard of the people around them. Sadly, many have lowered their standards for a mate for life just because they want to be happy now or because they want to make someone else happy. This is not the way to live a fulfilling life!

You, also, might be tempted to raise your expectations past the point of comfort simply to please someone else. You may be tempted to pursue a degree program in college that you do not like just because someone wants you to do it. You may be tempted to take on so many extra-curricular activities that will compete for your time and energy that you begin to suffer stress and depression. You need to learn to say, "No!" Don't give others the freedom to run your life for you. You should take charge of your life and manage it properly based on your own convictions.

Final Thoughts:
Expect Your Expectations to Be Challenged
John the baptizer was doing his work in the wilderness and the people came to him in great numbers. Along with those whose coming was honest and sincere, John "...saw many of the Pharisees and Sadducees coming to his baptism..." (Matthew3:7). You might be tempted to think that this was a wonderful moment in the preaching of John. Based on what you know about these leaders, you would not expect them to have appreciated John or taken the time to approach him.

However, their coming was not what you might have thought. John recognized immediately that he was being challenged. The challenge was to be proud that his preaching was having such a great effect among the Jewish leaders. Maybe he really was changing them!

However, he knew the real story behind these people. His response to the challenge was swift and clear. "Brood of vipers! Who warned you to flee from the wrath to come?" (Matthew 3:7). He demanded that they "bring forth fruits worthy of repentance" (Matthew 3:8). He even challenged their view of standing before the God of the universe, (Matthew 3:9-10). Finally, he warned them of the One to come whose judgment they would not escape unless they repent truly, (Matthew 3:11-12).

Expect Others to Come Along and Outshine You
You can do many great things in life. Greatness is doing what you can do to the best of your abilities. You might even do some things

greater than anyone else. Sometime, though, somewhere someone will come along and outshine even the best of us.

John the baptizer experienced this and, even, welcomed it! He called the one coming after him "mightier than I, whose sandals I am not worthy to carry" (Matthew 3:11). He proved these were not merely good-sounding words. When Jesus came to him and asked him to baptize Him, John's response was humble and submissive to his earlier words. The text states, "And John tried to prevent Him, saying, 'I need to be baptized by You, and are You coming to me?" (Matthew 3:14). John did not sulk and whine about someone stealing his spotlight. He did not use this encounter as an opportunity to brag that he was the one who baptized Jesus! John understood his place as preparatory for Jesus' work. That is the right attitude for you to have as you enter the rest of your life. You are setting the stage for someone or some others to build upon what you will do and raise the work to an even higher level.

There is no shame in others surpassing your accomplishments. The only shame would be if you are ashamed of your good accomplishments! You have a place to fill in the on-going history of this world. Fill it with vigor and vitality. Be proud when someone comes along and builds on what you have accomplished. They could not have built upon something if you had not laid down your part.

Prayer: *O Lord God of Heaven and Earth, I praise your name and offer you thanks for the many blessings you have given me. I pray that you will open doors of opportunity for me to use my talents to spread Your kingdom and to aid people in this life. Help me to hold onto high expectations for myself, never settling for just getting by. I ask for courage and strength to meet the challenges that will come as I pursue the course of my life. Help me not to give in to people who will try to divert my attention and my direction and I will give You the glory for whatever good I might accomplish in this life. In the name of Jesus the Christ, Amen.*

Brainstorming Ideas to Make this a Reality in Your Life:

1. Make a list of expectations that you have of yourself while you are away.

2. Review that list often to see how you are doing.

3. Have an accountability partner who knows what you expect of your-

self and will call you into account from time to time.

4. Thank your parents for expecting great things of you.

What other ideas do you have?
1.
2.
3.

Discussion Starters:

1. How can you be sure that your expectations of yourself are not too low?

2. How can you be sure that your expectations of yourself are not too high?

3. How should you respond to people who try to challenge your expectations of yourself?

4. What do you need to do to merge your spiritual expectations and your physical expectations of yourself, while keeping the spiritual ones the top priority?

CHAPTER 13
PRODIGAL SON: YOU CAN ALWAYS COME HOME, EVEN IF YOU MESS UP

Read the text: Luke 15:11-32

The Bible is filled with stories about people who messed up. Some failed to do what they agreed to do. Some did things they knew they should not do. There are accounts of people lying, stealing, cheating, and, even murdering. These stories are also about people who were identified as God's people! It is obvious, therefore, that people mess up. This is not a shocking revelation. While you are away from home, you are going to mess up. The question is not IF you will, but WHEN you will.

The story of the lost younger son, (Luke 15:11-32), is a fitting account of someone messing up, but, more importantly, coming home. It has been said that the measure of a person should not be based on how many times he or she falls, but rather, how many times they get up. There is no question that you are going to fall while you are away from home, but there should also be no question that you can come home whenever you choose. There certainly is no question whether God will take you back. So, how does a person come home when they have journeyed into the far country?

Come to Your Senses (Luke 15:17)

To come home, you have to come to your senses. This younger son had demanded, "Father, give me the portion of goods that falls to me" (Luke 15:12). The Bible then records that he "wasted his possessions with prodigal living" (Luke 15:13). This young man must have thought that he was so rich that he did not have to be concerned about the future. He did not consult a financial counselor. He did not visit a bank and open a savings account. He journeyed to a far country where he thought he could have a good time. I can just hear an older, seasoned citizen responding to this young man's choice, "Have you lost your mind?" The answer is, YES!

Though there was very little wise planning going on in his head, he had planned enough that this was not a spur-of-the-moment decision. He knew what he wanted and he pursued it with gusto. To no thinking person's surprise, he woke up one day and it was all gone! His pie-in-the-sky dream was now a nightmare. Whatever friends he had bought and paid for abandoned him, probably to find someone else to mooch off. The security he felt with all of that money rattling around in his pocket and the finest food he could afford in his stomach was replaced with the silent horror of empty pockets and the growling sound of an empty stomach.

The only thing he could find to do was work for a farmer feeding his pigs. Could things be any worse for a Jewish boy of privilege? He was living lower and eating worse than the slaves back home. He was so low that he actually thought he could eat the same slop the pigs were eating. Finally, "...he came to himself..." (Luke 15:17).

Have you ever heard the phrase, "You might have to reach the bottom before you will be able to climb back to the top"? There are some people who do not come to their senses until they reach the lowest point they can possibly reach. This young man was in just such a place. He was at the bottom and was ready to climb back to the top.

When you fail, you will be at a low point. Hopefully, you will come to your senses before you sink so low that you find yourself in real danger. How far down you have to go to come back to your senses, though, is how far you need to go to get there. No one ever comes home without feeling the weight of their poor decisions. You will not come home until you understand that what you thought was sensible at the time was really non-sense.

Come to a Decision (Luke 15:18)

To come home, you have to come to a decision. This young, lost boy was wallowing around in the muck and mire of a pig pen. Now, he was feeling the weight of the poor decisions he had made. He really had two options at this point. He could have chosen to sit in the pig pen and whine and complain. He could have blamed all the people he met in the far country for swindling him. He could have bemoaned all the people who claimed to be his friends, but turned out only to want his money.

To his credit, however, he did none of those things. He chose a different option; he made a rational decision in the midst of all the irrational ones he had been making. He said, "I will arise and go to my

While You Are Away From Home

father…" (Luke 15:18). That could not have been an easy decision. By making it, he knew he would have to face the music at home. He might be ridiculed, condemned, or shunned. This decision was all the more difficult because of all the things that had happened from his other poor decisions. However, it was the right one to make.

Someday you will find yourself in a position of needing to come home. It may not, (and, prayerfully, will not), be as bad a situation as this lost boy, but you will make some bad decisions that will put you in some difficult situations in the future. Determine now not to make things worse by merely whining and complaining without doing anything different. You will need to make a sensible decision and begin the process of coming home again.

Come to an Understanding (Luke 15:18-19)

To come home, you have to come to an understanding. The thing that made the decision so difficult for this boy was the need to admit the real problem. He, admittedly, had many problems. He had left home under less than ideal circumstances. He had wasted all his money. He had, apparently, engaged in some questionable or even sinful behaviors. He had made the wrong kinds of friends. And, now, he was sitting in a pig pen taking care of an animal that his Jewish heritage had told him was unclean and should be avoided.

This, however, was not his real problem. He stated his real problem, "Father, I have sinned against Heaven and before you" (Luke 15:18). Bad choices are not always sinful choices. So, bad choices were not the real problem. His problem was not a youthful indiscretion. He was not just "sowing wild oats", which is a phrase many use to minimize the seriousness of the deeds. He understood that he had sinned.

His sin was two-fold and he understood the proper order of offense necessary in order to come home properly. He knew, first, that he had sinned against Heaven. He had enough spiritual training to recognize that his main offense was against his God. This was a confession that verified he had not merely made poor decisions. Whatever he had done, (and we are not given details, except by his brother who had no direct knowledge), he admitted was sinful.

He had also sinned against his father. His sin had damaged his father's reputation. Perhaps you, too, were told by your father as I was, "Son, remember whose name you are wearing." His sin had created an environment in which contention arose in the family that need not have done so, (as the older son complained to his father about his own feelings

85

of mistreatment for so many years). His sin had caused grief and anguish for so long to his father. It seems that the father's habit had been to look for his son's return ever since he had gone away. The text does not tell us how long he was gone, but it does tell us that on the day the son came home the father was standing outside looking for him, maybe as he had done every day since the boy went away.

Now, this son was willing to face the consequences at home for the decisions he had made while he was away from home. He was going to admit that he did not deserve to be called the man's son. He was going to be content being a servant in his own home if he could just come home, (Luke 15:19).

You need to understand that there are consequences to the decisions we make in life. When you sin in the future, you will be forced to face the music. You will need to admit the sin, understanding its depth and the consequences that are sure to follow. However, this understanding should not keep you away from home. It is still far better, as the lost boy in the story understood, to face the consequences at home than to remain in the far country.

Come Home (Luke 15:20)

To come home, you have to come home. "And he arose and came to his father…" (Luke 15:20) This lost boy had to come to himself before he could come to his father. But, eventually, he had to come home to complete the rebuilding process. Coming to his senses, coming to a decision, and coming to an understanding would have been fruitless if he had not gotten up and come home. He could not repair the damage at home or in his own life while he was still in the far country.

The first step out of the pig pen had to be the hardest. Until this point, he was dealing only with himself. Stepping out of the pig pen was going to put him on the path to confronting others. He had rehearsed what he was going to say, but I'm sure he felt that no rehearsal time could prepare him to look into his father's face. His rehearsed words about being a servant were an expression not only of what he thought he deserved, but also what he thought he might actually get. He was prepared for the worst!

But, he found something entirely different. He faced a father who was glad to have him home! He felt the hug of the man he had run from! He found himself wearing the best robe in his father's house, (Luke 15:22), while he was still wearing the grime from pig pen. He was forgiven!

86   While You Are Away From Home

While you are away from home, you will face your own pig pens. Hopefully, most will be less intense than this boy found, but they will test your resolve to be the child of God that you want to be. You will have the option to come home when you run from your God. He will gladly welcome you home.

In the previous two stories in Luke 15:1-10, Jesus told about a lost sheep and a lost coin. He used the stories to make the point that anyone who is lost can come home. His words were the same in both instances. He said that there is joy in Heaven among the angels of God whenever a lost person comes home. It will not be easy to face the music, but it will be easier than facing further consequences of staying away. May God give you wisdom and strength to come home when you find that you are lost.

Brainstorming Ideas to Make this a Reality in Your Life:
1. Take an evaluation of yourself to see any areas of your life in which you have strayed from your home training and need to return.

2. Identify the basic habits that your parents have instilled in you and determine to keep them while you are away.

3. Write to your parents and thank them for having given you a good foundation to build on while you are away. Assure them that you know they will forgive you if you mess up.

What other ideas do you have?
1.
2.
3.

Discussion Starters:

1. Why is the far country such a draw to people while they are away from home?

2. What does repentance mean? What does it require from a person?

3. How are forgiveness from sin and consequences of sin different?

4. Why is repenting so difficult?

NOTES

_____

_____

_____

_____

_____

_____

_____

_____

_____

_____

_____

_____

_____

_____

_____

_____

While You Are Away From Home

NOTES

NOTES

_____

_____

_____

_____

_____

_____

_____

_____

_____

_____

_____

_____

_____

_____

_____

_____

_____

While You Are Away From Home

NOTES

70920852R00051

Made in the USA
Middletown, DE
18 April 2018